M000211285

KICKING TECHNIQUES

for
Competition
and
Self~Defense

KICKING TECHNIQUES
for Competition & Self~Defense

by
ROY KURBAN

© Ohara Publications, Incorporated 1979
All rights reserved
Printed in the United States of America
Library of Congress Catalog Card Number: 79-65639

ISBN 0-89750-065-2

Fourteenth printing 2003

Cover: Sergio Onaga

OHARA 🔲 PUBLICATIONS, INCORPORATED
SANTA CLARITA, CALIFORNIA

DEDICATION

I wish to express my deep appreciation to my friends Steve Fisher, John Conroy, and Ronnie Ramsey who left busy schedules to assist with the photographs. I want to thank Sandy Blauvelt for the beautiful cover photo of Ronnie and me, and the staff at Ohara Publications for their special assistance.

—R.K.

I have been involved with the development of Roy Kurban's kicking techniques since the early 60s. His ability to demonstrate and instruct the kicking techniques which made him an international champion are vividly displayed in his book. Roy's proven ability to apply these advanced kicking techniques in real situations should make his book required reading for all martial artists.

—Larry Caster

When it comes to enhancing your knowledge and improving your skills confidence, this book is a must. I know Mr. Kurban's championship skills to be a masterful invitation for anyone interested in surpassing the boundaries which prevent us all from becoming champions. I know from personal ring experience with Roy Kurban that the contents of this book have been field tested!

—Joe Lewis

I make this book mandatory reading for all my students and all black belts who train with me.

—Steve Fisher

I've read Roy Kurban's book, and it's fantastic, a valuable tool for a martial artist at any level!...a must for your library. Do yourself a favor and get it!

—Mike Stone

I'm prejudiced in favor of this book because Roy Kurban helped me develop my kicking strategy in the early 70s. *Kicking Techniques for Competition and Self-Defense* is required reading at my studio.

—Dennis "Sugar Bear" Gotcher

This is the only book that I recommend for my students to read to improve their kicking techniques.

—Jim Harrison

Roy Kurban was one of the finest competitors of the late 60s and through the mid-70s. He is an excellent instructor. This book is a must for a person who wants to learn to fight.

—Bill Wallace

Thirty-four years ago I was taught karate on Okinawa by Master Seikichi Toguchi. I was taught kicking in Texas by Master Roy Kurban. His book on kicking should be bought, studied, and used by martial artists of all styles.

—Shodai Jay Trombley,
Founder of United Goju Ryu

After having been on the receiving end of Roy Kurban's kicks, I can promise you that this is a valuable book for all martial artists.

—Jeff Smith

FOREWORD

Roy Kurban's *KICKING TECHNIQUES FOR COMPETITION AND SELF-DEFENSE* is throughout a straightforward series of illustrated descriptions, a setting forth of techniques that made him one of the top tournament fighters all during the middle '70s and make him one of the most popular instructors in Texas karate today. If Ohara were in the business of publishing directories instead of martial arts books, no doubt this foreword would be dispensed with in favor of running through an unadorned list of his achievements—for example, the 115 tournaments he placed in between 1968 and 1976. Suffice it to say that he won 44 of those, taking eight grand championships and 29 first places for kata. In short, these techniques worked for Roy Kurban.

Flowery, philosophical books call for flowery, philosophical forewords. Reversing that logic and applying it to this book, it is clear that very spare, plain language should be used here. This book is not awash in philosophy or opinion. Nor does it seek to unearth or illuminate keys and paths by which any 90-pound weakling can destroy opponents after only two weeks' training.

But enough already. If you aren't convinced by now that Roy Kurban's experience is his own best advertising for his book, pick up some old issues of a martial arts magazine. If you are, read on; in *KICK TO WIN*, kicks and punches are set forth by somebody who has delivered a lot of them.

BASIC STANCE DEFINITIONS

Open stance refers to a position in which two fighters face the same direction, each having the opposite foot closest to his opponent. Closed stance refers to a position in which two fighters face opposite directions, each having the

BASIC STANCE 1

INTRODUCTION

This book concentrates on the development of the intermediate and advanced students of the martial arts. The specific aim of *KICKING TECHNIQUES FOR COMPETITION AND SELF-DEFENSE* is to show the reader how to make a kick faster, stronger and more effective; it does not deal with the fundamentals of kicking. The concepts that are presented did not evolve from any single system of the martial arts. The ideas on kicking were learned from good teachers, through competition and from personal observations.

The primary thrust of this book deals with the detailed application of kicks, although punching techniques, which increase the effectiveness of the kicking maneuver, are demonstrated.

All of the techniques that are given in this book are functional in both competition and self-defense. I have personally executed all of them successfully, and I know many others who now employ these same combinations in tournament competition. Although many head-high kicks are included in this book, the value of these kicks for self-defense purposes has been a point of heated

same foot closest to his opponent. The principle of offsetting balance refers to the fighter's position, open or closed stance, in which the two opponents do not share the same centerline of balance.

BASIC STANCE 2

argument among martial artists. The fighter who is capable of kicking to the head with speed and power possesses an extra weapon in his arsenal. Concentrated training on the powerful, high-kicking techniques serves to increase the speed and power of low-kicking attacks.

This book has been designed specifically as a training aid, and several of the key concepts are frequently repeated only to emphasize their importance. The training sessions may be modified to suit the individual's time schedule. To gain the maximum benefits from this book, some suggestions should be offered. First, read through a few pages at a time, paying close attention to details. Study closely the photographs of a single technique, then practice this technique until you acquire a thorough understanding of the concept and develop a feel for the movement. Do not move on to another technique until you feel that you have mastered the one that you are working on. Remember, repetition is the key to success.

—Roy D. Kurban

ABOUT THE AUTHOR

Roy Kurban enrolled in tae kwon do classes at Allen Street's Texas Karate Institute in 1965. Earning the coveted black belt in 1968, he initiated a martial sports career which has spanned four decades. A two-year tour of duty with the United States Army from 1969 until 1971 included a one-year assignment in Seoul, South Korea, where Kurban trained under Grandmaster Won Chik Park. A strong student-instructor relationship emerged which endures to this day. After Kurban was honorably discharged from the military in 1971, he resumed his competitive career, producing a total of 127 awards in forms and fighting. *Black Belt* magazine and *Karate Illustrated* ranked Kurban among the top ten fighters in the United States from 1972 through 1976. In 1975, Roy entered the fledgling sport of kickboxing, fighting for Chuck Norris' National Karate League. Through the coaching efforts of Larry Caster and a total commitment to training, Kurban achieved a world ranking as a lightweight in 1975 and 1976.

Kurban retired from tournament competition in 1976, and redirected his efforts to promoting karate tournaments, kickboxing events, and officiating at martial sports events across the nation. In 1982, he joined forces with Frank Babcock, Fred Wren, Larry Caster, and Bob Wall to organize the Karate International Council of Kickboxing (KICK). Chuck Norris accepted the role as KICK's goodwill ambassador, and the sanctioning body has grown into one of the largest, most prestigious organizations of its kind.

Kurban's vocation as a martial arts instructor has been the foundation of all of his competitive and promotional efforts. Throughout a teaching career which was inaugurated in 1967, he has instructed military personnel, FBI and U.S. Treasury agents, and police officers. Kurban opened the doors of his dojang in 1973 in Arlington, Texas. He continues to teach defensive tactics to local police agencies, but invests most of his time teaching and training students at his American Black Belt Academy.

In 1988, Kurban earned his Peace Officer Certification from the State of Texas, and worked as a member of a tactical drug enforcement team for the Dalworthington Gardens Department of Public Safety until 1990. Kurban relied upon his martial arts expertise and discipline to assist him in handling potentially life-threatening situations which occurred during forced entry, high-risk drug raids, and felony warrant service.

After a 13-year retirement from the ring, Kurban returned to tournament competition in 1989 to re-test the techniques which served him so well during the campaigns of the '60s and '70s. He won the 1989 and 1990 heavyweight black belt division of the Texas State Police Olympics. In August 1989, Kurban traveled to Ed Parker's International Karate Championships in Los Angeles, where he joined with Steve Fisher, John Natividad, Dennis Gotcher, and Duane Magett to capture the black belt Master's Team Championship.

Kurban's life in the martial arts has been distinguished by a number of significant awards. In 1975, he was introduced on the floor of the Texas Senate, where he was commended for "his diligence and perseverance in mastering the ancient discipline of tae kwon do." That same year he won the Arlington Boys Club Outstanding Service Award for sponsoring fund-raising karate tournaments for disadvantaged youths. In 1981, Kurban was inducted into the *Black Belt* Hall of Fame as "Man of the Year." He was promoted to sixth-degree black belt by the World Tae Kwon Do Federation in an exam conducted by his instructor, Grandmaster Won Chik Park in August 1986. He also earned the Master Instructor Certification from the World Tae Kwon Do Federation (1980).

In 1990, Kurban turned his attention to the political arena, defeating an incumbent judge. Kurban serves as Justice of the Peace in Tarrant County, Texas, hearing civil and criminal cases. His venue consists of eight cities and more than 200,000 citizens.

CONTENTS

PUNCHING STANCE

STANCES

The best possible stance for kicking is one which:
1. Makes possible maximum utilization of both legs;
2. Is a catalyst for explosive forward motion, quick sidestepping and rapid, balanced retreat;
3. Is conducive to easy and rapid shifting of weight from foot to foot;
4. Employs a light, continuous shuffling movement rather than the wide and fixed traditional stance.

The effective fighter makes the most of his kicking potential by possessing a dynamic punching attack. But an effective punching stance eliminates a large variety of kicking technique, just as a strong kicking stance restricts total punching mobility. The thinking fighter, therefore, will employ continuous movement and shift

KICKING STANCE **TRADITIONAL STANCE**

back and forth from the punching to the kicking position.

The puncher obviously adheres to the stance and movement most advantageous to his game. He will point both of his feet in the direction of his opponent while twisting his body to a 45-degree angle from his opponent. In this position, both hips and hands may be thrown efficiently.

The best kicking stance is one in which the fighter turns either side to his opponent, pointing his toes from a 45- to a 90-degree angle away from his opponent. An attempt to arrive at a fixed stance from which to throw kicks and punches will severely limit a fighter's potential in both areas, but by maintaining the strategy of a constant shuffle between two stances, a fighter can initiate either a punching or kicking attack whenever the opportunity presents itself.

BASIC KICKING

A good martial artist views a kicking technique in the same light he views a punching, elbow or knee technique. The kicking technique is a tool of self-defense or competition to be used at the right moment for a particular purpose. The kicking technique is employed to strike an opponent who is *out of punching range*. Its obvious usage is for an opponent who:

1. has retreated from punching range;
2. has attacked inside kicking range but outside punching range;
3. is maintaining a neutral, defensive position within kicking distance but outside punching range.

The kick is perhaps the most misunderstood technique of the martial arts. People inside and outside the martial arts can easily see the advantages of kicking over punching. Kicking is a surprise weapon on the street. Kicking is much more powerful than punching, and the reach of the leg is far greater than the arm. The majority of people in the martial arts do not possess the true knowledge of how to kick, when to kick and where to kick! This lack of knowledge may be attributed to a weakness in the training method. Although the advantages of a strong kicking maneuver are obvious, many fighters overlook the responsibility of long hours of arduous stretching, coordination drills, form work, bag work, running and the weight training required to master the kicking tool. It is much more difficult to attain control over legs than arms, and this fact calls for the martial artist to spend more training time on kicking techniques than punching. Do not misconstrue the last statement to mean that kicking is more important than punching. Total development of both skills is essential to the fighter. "The hammer and saw are two irreplaceable tools of the carpenter."

Outside of vigorous and thorough kicking drills and exercises, one of the best methods of developing a dynamic kicking attack is

to possess a strong punching combination. If your opponent re-
spects your punching ability, his attention will be drawn away
from your kicking technique. His distraction will become his
downfall and your victory.

DECEPTION IN KICKING

Deception in kicking is achieved in three ways:
1. Disguising a kicking attack with a punching technique;
2. Not committing yourself to your kick until the last possible
second;
3. Combining the above two methods to form the third: make
your opponent believe you are going to do one thing and do
another.

EXTENDED KNEE FOLD

(1A) Application of extended knee fold drawing opponent's vision to the moving knee away from the kicking foot.

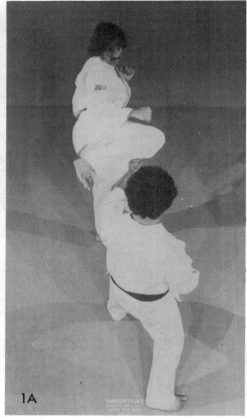

1A

DECEPTION in the FOLD

The proficient kicker possesses the ability to execute several kicks from the same fold. All karateka are taught a separate fold for each individual kick. Initial karate training demands this method of instruction, so as to prevent confusion in the mind of the beginner.

As the skill of the karateka increases, he develops the ability to associate a particular kick with a certain fold. Obviously, it would be extremely beneficial to disguise a kick within the fold itself. Throughout this text, a continuous emphasis has been placed on maintaining a constant head height, hiding rear leg motion with

RETRACTED KNEE FOLD

(2A) Application of the retracted knee fold is to hide the initial fold of the kick behind your opponent's shoulder. Your opponent's line of vision is obscured by your position and his own shoulder.

2A

the front and concealing kicking intentions with distracting punching attacks. Developing the skill to execute several kicks from the same fold, the fighter adds a new dimension to his striking potential. The roundhouse kick, heel kick, and side kick are three techniques which may be easily thrown from the same basic fold. In this fold, the kicking thigh is positioned parallel to the ground. The calf muscle should remain lightly tensed, the heel drawn back as close to the thigh as possible, and the toes of the kicking foot drawn back toward the knee. The heel of the supporting foot should point in the direction of one's opponent to allow max-

GENERAL (OR DECEPTIVE) FOLD

ROUNDHOUSE KICK EXTENDED FROM DECEPTIVE FOLD POSITION

imum use of one's hips and leg extension.

Within this 'deceptive fold' exist two basic knee positions, the extended knee fold and retracted knee fold. In the extended knee fold, the shin of the kicking leg will bisect the centerline of the kicker's balance. The retracted knee fold places the knee of the kicking leg directly on the centerline of the kicker's balance.

Both knee positions elicit different reactions from an opponent. The extended knee position may be applied in either the open or closed stance. This position disrupts an opponent's timing because his attention will be directed to the motion of your knee rather

INITIATION OF HEEL
KICK FROM DECEP-
TIVE FOLD POSITION

SIDE EXTENDED
FROM DECEPTIVE
FOLD POSITION

than the foot moving behind the knee. The function of the retracted knee fold is to *conceal* kicking motion. The retracted fold is
used in the open stance, and the principle advantage is achieved by
assuming the offsetting balance position to your opponent's back.

The basic concept of the deceptive fold is "to make your opponent believe that you are going to throw one kick, and then throw
another." The following series of photographs will illustrate how
you trick your opponent into blocking a kick that never material-
izes. These photographs should help the reader develop ideas for
his own techniques.

STRETCHING:
DEVELOPING SPEED

Stretching is the key to the fast kick. Pliable, loose muscles are fast muscles. In fact, stretching must be considered the single most important aspect in developing kicking ability. Not only does stretching increase speed, it improves muscle control (consequently, the accuracy of kicking technique) and expands the range of motion of the legs. Assuming the majority of people who read this book will be aware of the wide variety of stretching exercises, I will not go into standard drills.

The following two-man drills, however, are highly beneficial when used to supplement individual stretching exercises. The exercises are simple and yet very effective. Remember that at least 30

minutes a day should be set aside for stretching—five to six days a week. Never force a stretching position to the point of extreme discomfort. Work slowly and patiently.

Another beneficial tool which may be discussed as a stretching drill is "slow kicking." Using a stretching bar or even a wall for support, a stretching of muscles can be achieved by holding a slowly executed kick at full extension for 10 to 20 seconds. This is repeated five times with each leg. The front kick, roundhouse and side kick are all executed in this manner. For placing additional stress on the stretching muscles, straighten the supporting leg. (In the actual execution of the kick, the supporting leg always remains bent.)

STRETCHING DRILL #1

(1) Sit on the floor with both of your feet straight in front, legs locked at the knee. (2) Grab your ankles and pull your head to your knees gently. (3) After holding your head to the knees for 30 to 60 seconds, have a partner push lightly on your back for an additional 60 seconds. Repeat the exercise two more times. If you cannot pull your head all the way to the knees, pull to the point of "mildly uncomfortable" extension.

STRETCHING DRILL #2

(1) Sit on the floor, spreading your legs as wide as possible. (2) Grab your ankles and gently pull your head as close to the floor as possible. (3) After 30 to 60 seconds of continuous pressure, have your partner gently push on your back for an additional 60 seconds. Repeat the exercise two more times.

STRETCHING DRILL #3: TWO-MAN SPLITS

(1) Execute the splits to the side by yourself for 60 seconds. Point your toes up and to the outside to prevent knee strain. Place one hand in front of your body and one behind. Gradually bounce your hips down to increase the pressure on your muscles. (2) Have a partner grab you around the chest and under the arms while placing his shins behind your thighs. (This prevents the legs from moving, keeping pressure on the muscles.) (3) Your partner should lower you slowly to your maximum stretch and hold for 60 seconds.

DEVELOPING FORM
of the KICK

The proper form of any kick is the most efficient method of its execution. Efficiency in kicking implies speed, power and effectiveness. Therefore, a crucial factor in the development of kicking skill is the concentrated effort to improve the form of the kick.

Each kick may be divided into its three principal parts: the initial move, the fold and the snap or execution of the kick. Through repetitious practice of the individual segments of the kick, the efficiency of the entire kick is increased.

FRONT VIEW

The initial move is the slowest part of the kick. To improve the delivery speed of a kick thrown from the rear leg, practice sliding the rear foot slightly ahead of the front. Concentrate on increasing speed with each stance change. For an explosive kick from the front leg, snap the rear foot to the front. Maintain a constant head height, and hide the movement of the rear leg with the front. The initial move will be quicker if the legs are already in motion.

SIDE VIEW

The second part of the kick, the fold, requires flexible leg muscles. Numerous repetitions increase speed.

2

3

2

3

After the initial motion and folding drills have been executed, combine the two segments and create a third drill.

Snapping the foot from the fold is the fastest part of the kick. Fold the leg tightly and attempt to keep the calf muscles relaxed. Practice kicking from the fold position, concentrating on the *completion* of the snap.

After practicing the various parts of a kick, begin training with the entire kicking motion. When not striking a bag, be careful not

to hyperextend your knees by locking each kick at full extension in a full-power motion. Concentrate on fold and speed rather than power when working for form. Hard kicks should be saved for the bag. Repetition is the key to developing a proper feel for the kick. There is no other substitute. The serious martial artist executes from 250 to 1,000 form kicks a day.

TRAINING: DEVELOPING POWER in the KICK

Running, bag work and weight lifting are the three primary methods used for developing power in the kicking attack.

RUNNING

The two techniques of running—sprinting and distance running —serve to develop the kicking power in separate areas. Distance running provides stamina and increased endurance for executing a quantity of kicks. Sprinting contributes an explosive quality to the initial movement and snap. Before running, always take time to warm up and stretch to prevent pulling muscles. A minimum warm-up period of 10 minutes is suggested. On completion of a run, always engage in another stretching session to prevent the muscles from tightening. A good training schedule demands six days per week of running. Alternate drills from day to day—one day, sprinting; the next, distance running.

On the day of the sprinting drill, warm up and jog an easy mile to totally prepare for hard work. Run 10 to 20 50-yard sprints as

hard as you possibly can. On completion of each run, jog backwards on the balls of the feet all the way back to your starting point to keep the muscles warm and loose.

Run two or three miles. Every time you run, attempt to improve your time. The basic idea is to raise your level of endurance and strength by making your body work harder and harder.

There are a few important items that must be remembered:
1. Stretch thoroughly before and after each run.
2. Keep your body warm during running drills. It is best to wear a sweatsuit.
3. Pick some excellent track shoes for running. Poor shoes can damage feet, knees and back.
4. Use an analgesic balm (heat) to help keep the muscles warm and loose.

BAG TRAINING

The heavy bag is the indispensable tool of the powerful kicker. Through hard bag training, the fighter develops power, stamina,

Speed, timing and an all-important feel for contact. The bag brings a taste of the reality of the match or fight to the karateka. The difference between snapping a kick in the air for practice and hitting a resisting object is as different as night and day!

A thorough warm-up and stretching period before engaging in a brisk session of bag work is essential. An initial warm-up session on the bag itself is recommended to get a feel for the contact. Light to moderate power should be used in your kicks at first to make sure that the muscles are ready. When satisfied with initial, light bag contact, begin the hard bag training.

Start your session with the bag in a still position. Using both legs, execute five to 10 repetitions of each kick. Repeat the same drill again, but this time swing the bag. By kicking the moving bag, you develop the ability to time a rushing opponent. Do not favor the development of one leg over the other. To be a truly versatile fighter, you need equal kicking ability with both legs. Practice kicking the bag from both fixed and moving stances. Each time you kick, make sure to exhale forcefully from the diaphragm. This will increase your power and help regulate breathing, developing greater endurance.

After completing a drill, having concentrated on your individual kicking techniques, engage in a freestyle kicking exercise. Move freely around the bag, executing spontaneous combinations, letting the position of the bag dictate the technique. Keep the bag swinging and keep yourself shuffling on the balls of your feet. During the freestyle period, kick the bag in two-minute rounds. Between each round, take a one-minute stretching period to keep the muscles loose.

Three or five 30-minute workouts on the bag a week are recommended. Increased desire to excel will, of course, require yet more time on the bag.

WEIGHT TRAINING

Weight training is a proven method for increasing the strength in the muscles. An increase in the muscle strength of the legs obviously produces greater kicking power. A thorough warm-up before and after weight lifting drills prevents pulled muscles. The importance of stretching cannot be overemphasized! Another aspect to consider while weight training is proper breathing. Inhale on preparation to lift, exhale during the execution of the exercise.

I personally recommend the Universal Weight Machine as an excellent training tool for quick, effective results that provide a high degree of safety. Each exercise should be performed in three sets of 10 repetitions, with a 60-second stretching exercise of your choice between sets. After you lift the weight to the peak of extension, return to the beginning position slowly. Take care when beginning a weight-lifting program. Choose a weight for each exercise that taxes your strength, but not one that you cannot handle. Begin gradually. Three excellent exercises for developing power are the leg press, thigh extension and leg curl.

KICKING TECHNIQUES

FRONT SNAP KICK

FRONT SNAP KICK: OPEN STANCE

(1&2) Draw your opponent's attention from your kicking attack by initiating a backfist to his head. (3&4) Following with a reverse punch to the head, slide the back foot to the front. (Do not lift the rear foot from the ground until it has passed the front foot.) (5—7) Initiate a front snap kick with the sliding foot directly from the ground to your opponent's groin. (Do not allow your head height to vary as it divides your power in two directions and alerts your opponent to your attack.)

ROUNDHOUSE KICKS

DEFENSIVE ROUNDHOUSE TO THE GROIN: CLOSED STANCE

(1) Using the principle of offsetting balance, adjust your balance so that the front foot is behind your opponent's, not on a straight line with his foot. Shuffling movement can create this advantageous position for you. (2) Begin the initial snap of the kick from the ground; do not fold the kick so as to draw your opponent's attention to your technique. Lift the kicking foot behind your opponent's centerline of balance. Use the position of your opponent's front defensive hand to hide your initial motion from his attention. (Maintain a constant head height and facial expression throughout initial execution so as to conceal your intentions.) (3) Snap the instep into your opponent's groin, thrusting your weight forward. (4&5) Complete the technique by trapping your opponent's front hand with your rear hand. (6—8) Follow with a front hand hook or ridgehand technique. The kick has served as a jabbing and distraction technique to set up the follow-through.

DEFENSIVE ROUNDHOUSE TO THE HEAD: OPEN STANCE

(1) Using the principle of offsetting balance, adjust your balance to your opponent's by placing both your feet behind the centerline of your opponent's balance. (2&3) Begin the kick behind your opponent, folding the kicking leg instantly as it leaves the ground. Roll the hip over so that the thigh and calf of the leg are parallel to the ground. Do not lean back, move your hands or change facial expression. (4) Snap either the ball of the foot or instep into your opponent's jaw, carotid artery or base of the skull. Simultaneously, slip the supporting foot forward. (5—7) After returning the kick to fold, snap a hard roundhouse kick to the lower area of your opponent's calf, sweeping him to the ground. (8—9) Complete with stomping or punching attack. The defensive roundhouse in this instance serves two purposes: as a jab to stun your opponent, and as a sweep to destroy his balance to set up the *coup de grace!*

THE OFFENSIVE ROUNDHOUSE KICK: OPEN STANCE

(1&2) Initiate the attack with a backfist. (3) Follow with a reverse punch to the head, drawing his defense and attention to his own upper torso. (4&5) The rear foot immediately follows the punching technique but clings to the ground until it has passed the supporting foot. (6) Roll the hip over until thigh and calf are parallel to the ground. (7) Drive the ball of the foot into the solar plexus or groin. *(Remember:* Maintain a constant head height.) (8-10) As your opponent doubles over, drive a vertical chop with your rear hand to the base of his skull.

2

3

5

6

9

10

OFFENSIVE ROUNDHOUSE KICK: CLOSED STANCE

(1&2) Set up your opponent by splitting his defensive abilities. Fake a backfist strike to the head. (3&4) Fake a lunge punch to the body, drawing your opponent's hand down to stop your punch. (5&6) When your rear foot passes your supporting foot on the lunge-punch fake, snap the kicking foot into action by rolling the hip until thigh and calf are parallel to the ground. (7) Snap the ball of the foot into the temple, carotid arteries, or jaw (the instep may be used to the base of the skull). (8) Snap kick back. (9) Renew balance.

STEP-ACROSS
ROUNDHOUSE KICK:
CLOSED STANCE

(1—3) Draw your opponent's attention with a backfist strike to the head. (4&5) Follow the backfist attack with a reverse punch to the body. (6&7) Simultaneously step with your rear foot and drive a ridgehand technique to your opponent's nose with your front hand as you step. a) Maintain constant head height. b) Bring the stepping foot ahead of the front foot, keeping the moving leg as close to the supporting leg as possible. This will help disguise your intentions. (8) As you raise your leg, fold to kick. (9) Snap the kick into your opponent's groin or solar plexus. Rotate the hip to place your thigh and calf in a position parallel to the ground. (10&11) Return to original fold and prepare a follow-up if necessary.

50

SIDE KICKS

DEFENSIVE SIDE KICK: STANCE OPTIONAL

The defensive side kick is a tremendously powerful weapon for use against a highly aggressive opponent, but a great deal of timing skill is required to use the kick effectively. (1&2) As the opponent begins the attack, retreat with your front foot—sliding it over the ground until it makes contact with your rear foot. Do not change head height, facial expression, or move the upper part of the body while executing the stance change. (When watching for your attacker's initial move, *do not* concentrate on the eyes. Watch for shoulder, hip and general upper body motion as the key to impending attack.) (3) As the retreating foot makes contact with the supporting foot, instantly twist your hips toward the attacker. (4&5) Fold the retreating leg tightly, tucking the knee up into your stomach as though to throw a front kick in the opposite direction from which the attack is coming. (6&7) Drive the heel of the foot into your opponent's groin or solar plexus. For maximum commitment of weight and hips, keep the kneecap facing the ground. (8) Withdraw the kick to fold in case you need to strike again. Remember to keep the supporting leg bent throughout the execution of the kick.

DEFENSIVE SIDE KICK AGAINST AN EXTREMELY FAST ATTACKER

(1&2) As the opponent begins the attack, retreat with your front foot —sliding it over the ground until it makes contact with your rear foot. Do not change head height, facial expression, or move the upper part of the body while executing the stance change. (When watching for your attacker's initial move, do not concentrate on the eyes. Watch for shoulder, hip and general upper body motion as the key to his attack.) (3) As the retreating foot makes contact with the supporting foot, instantly twist your hips toward the attacker. (4) Slide the foot of the retreating leg to the ankle. (5) Drive the kick in a straight line to your opponent's groin or solar plexus. For maximum commitment of weight and hips, keep the kneecap facing the ground. (6&7) Quickly withdraw the kick to the initial fold and prepare to strike again if necessary. Remember to keep the supporting leg bent throughout the entire execution of the kick.

OFFENSIVE SIDE KICK: CLOSED STANCE

(1&2) Distract your opponent with a backfist to his head. (3&4) Follow with a lunge punch to the head. As you move forward with the rear foot, slide your rear leg as close to the supporting leg as possible. Make sure that you maintain a constant head height. (5) As your rear foot passes the supporting foot, twist your hips toward your opponent. Keep your head straight forward and attempt to keep your upper body as motionless as possible. (6) Fold the kicking foot to the supporting knee. (7&8) Thrust the heel of the kicking foot into your opponent's groin, solar plexus, or rib cage—depending on the availability of the target. (9&10) Snap heel back to fold. Return to initial position and prepare to follow up if necessary.

1

4

7

8

SLIDING SIDE KICK: OPEN STANCE

(1) Initiate your attack with a back-fist to your opponent's face as you (2) slide the back foot to your front foot. Keep your feet in line so that the front leg will hide the rear leg action. keep the head height the same, and make sure that there is as little upper body motion as possible. This will make it difficult for your opponent to time your attack. (3) As the back foot touches the front foot, immediately following the execution of the backfist, fold the front foot to upper calf. (4) The fold to the calf implies no hesitation, for the foot never stops moving. (5) Extend the kick directly into your opponent's ribs. Just before the kick makes contact, twist your hip so that the kneecap turns down and the heel comes up. This last twist will assist the penetration of the heel into your opponent's body. (5-8) Return kicking foot to the fold. Renew ready position and prepare for opponent's reaction.

TURN KICKS

OFFENSIVE TURN KICK: CLOSED STANCE

(1—3) Draw your opponent's guard up with a backfist to his head. At the same time, draw the rear foot to the front foot. Keep head height constant, and conceal the motion of the back foot with the front leg. (4&5) The instant the rear leg reaches the front, twist the hips while attempting to maintain the original upper body position—keeping the posture erect. (6—8) Maintaining the flow of initial motion, twist the head to view your opponent and snap your leg from the ground into your opponent's groin, solar plexus or ribs. (9&10) Snap kick back to fold and prepare for follow-up.

DEFENSIVE TURN KICK: CLOSED STANCE

(1&2) As your opponent attacks, retreat with the front foot; slide the foot back—do not step. Keep your head height the same. (3&4) As the front foot reaches the back foot, shift your weight to the front foot and twist your hips toward your opponent. (5—7) Snap the rear foot from the ground into your opponent's groin, solar plexus or ribs. (8&9) Return kick to fold and prepare for follow-up.

DEFENSIVE TURN KICK
AGAINST A
FAST ATTACKER:
CLOSED STANCE

(1&2) As your opponent attacks, retreat with the front
foot. (3) Take the retreating
foot a full stance-length past the
rear foot. (4&5) Shifting the
weight to the retreating foot,
draw the rear foot away from
the attacking opponent until it
reaches the supporting foot.
Maintain constant head height.
(6) Snap the heel of the rear
foot into your opponent's groin,
solar plexus or ribs. (7&8) Your
opponent's momentum will add
to the impact. Be sure to snap
the kicking leg back to fold
quickly.

2

3

5

6

8

HEEL KICKS

OFFENSIVE HEEL KICK: CLOSED STANCE

(1&2) Focus your opponent's attention on your upper body by attacking with a backfist to his head.

(3&4) Follow the backfist with a lunge punch to the body. As you slide through with the rear foot, keep your rear leg close to the supporting leg so as to conceal movement and increase speed of stance-change. (5) As the rear foot clears the front foot, roll the hip in order to shift the rear foot to the front position. Keep the foot close to the ground and maintain constant head height. (6) Continuing the motion, snap the kick in an arc toward your opponent's head. (7) Snap your heel into the base of your opponent's skull. (8) Snap the kick back to a fold, by attempting to drive your heel into your own thigh. (9) Return the kicking foot to the stance and prepare to follow up.

SLIDING OR STEP-UP HEEL KICK: OPEN STANCE

(1) Using the principle of offsetting balance, position yourself behind your opponent. Your feet should not be in line with your opponent's. (2) Initiate an attack with a backfist strike, simultaneously sliding your back foot to the front. A constant head height is necessary. (3) As the back foot slides to the front foot, shift your weight to the rear foot. The front foot instantly leaves the ground. (4) Begin the initial move of the kick behind your opponent's back. Attempt to keep your posture erect. (5) At waist level, snap the kicking leg in front of your opponent. (6&7) Drive the heel of the kicking leg into your opponent's face. Alternate targets may be solar plexus or groin. (8) Snap kick back to fold; drive the heel of the kicking foot back to your thigh. (9) Return kicking leg to the ground.

2

3

5

6

8

9

BACK SPINNING HEEL KICK: OPEN STANCE

(1&2) Attack your opponent with a backfist to the face, simultaneously sliding the back foot to the front. (3—5) Twist your hips toward the opponent and slide the back foot past the front while shifting your weight to the front foot. Twist your head to view your opponent's position and reaction instantly. (6&7) By making a tight arc, raise the kicking foot behind your opponent's back. (8) Snap the heel of the kicking foot into the base of your opponent's skull. (9) Snap your kicking heel into your thigh, thus completing the full motion of the kick. (10) Return kick to the ground.

DEFENSIVE HEEL KICK: CLOSED STANCE

(1—3) As your opponent attacks, sidestep with the rear foot (right foot sidesteps to the right, left foot sidesteps to the left). This maneuver will put you toward your opponent's back. (4&5) Arc the kicking heel into your opponent's neck, relying upon a hard roll of the hips and a snapping of the heel back to the kicking thigh to develop power. (6-8) Snap kicking heel into your thigh. Return kick to ground.

DEFENSIVE BACK
SPINNING HEEL KICK:
OPEN STANCE

(1&2) In a left foot forward stance, retreat from your opponent's attack by sliding your front foot back and around your rear foot. (3) Having pivoted on your right foot shift your weight to your left foot and whip your head around and check your opponent's position. (4&5) Raise your right foot and drive your heel into your opponent's head. (6&7) Return the kicking foot to the ground and prepare for a follow-up.

KICKING COMBINATIONS

FRONT KICK LOW —
ROUNDHOUSE KICK HIGH:
OPEN STANCE

(1&2) Slide the rear foot toward the front, holding a constant head height. (3—5) As the rear foot passes the front, execute a front snap kick with the instep—directly into your opponent's groin. (6) When the kick is blocked or scores, instantly snap back to a tight, vertical fold. (7) Rolling the hip and twisting the heel of the supporting foot toward your opponent, (8&9) snap a spin-kick to your opponent's face with either your instep or ball of foot. (10) Snap kicking foot back to fold. Return kicking foot to ground.

1

4

7

8

FRONT KICK LOW —
ROUNDHOUSE KICK HIGH:
CLOSED STANCE

(1&2) Slide the rear foot to the front, maintaining a constant head height. (3—5) Drive the instep of the kicking foot into the back of the knee while slightly rolling the hip. (6—8) After damaging your opponent's balance, snap your kicking foot back to a horizontal fold, and drive your heel into your thigh to assume a tight fold. (9) Snap a spin-kick to the base of your opponent's skull, employing your instep as the striking weapon. (10) Return your kick to the horizontal fold with the same force that you delivered it. (11) Return to initial position.

1

4

5

8

9

HIGH KNEE — ROUNDHOUSE KICK: OPEN STANCE

(1&2) Draw the rear foot to the front, keeping the moving foot on the ground until it reaches the front. (3) Draw your opponent's attention to your kicking knee by raising it to the highest vertical position possible. Make sure head height does not change as you move into the fold position. (4-6) Snap your leg in a "front kick motion fake" and twist your hip over as your opponent's hand drops, and snap the instep of your kicking foot into your opponent's nose. Return kick to horizontal fold. (7) Quickly assume fighting stance and prepare for follow-up.

2

4

5

7

HIGH KNEE —
ROUNDHOUSE KICK:
CLOSED STANCE

(1&2) Slide the rear foot to the front, shifting your weight to the front foot. (3) Pull the kicking knee to the highest vertical position possible. Your opponent should sense impending attack to his rib cage. (4) Snap your leg in a "front kick motion fake" and (5) twist your hip over and, as your opponent's front hand moves to block, (6) snap the ball of your foot into your opponent's jaw. (7&8) Explosively snap your kick back to the horizontal fold. Return to fighting stance.

FRONT KICK LOW —
HEEL KICK HIGH:
OPEN STANCE

(1&2) Slide your rear foot to the front foot. (3) Raise rear foot to the supporting leg's knee, folding kicking thigh parallel to the ground. (4) Snap a hard front kick to the groin and simultaneously throw kicking hip in front of supporting hip. (5) Snap to fold while turning leg and hip to a 45-degree angle. (6) Drop kicking foot below your opponent's knee while moving leg behind your opponent's back. (7) Arc a heel kick toward your opponent's head. While rotating your hip and shifting the kneecap toward the ground, pivot on the supporting foot. (8&9) Drive your heel into the opponent's neck. (10) Follow through the arc of the kick by snapping the heel into your own thigh. Return to initial stance.

1

4

7

8

FAKE ROUNDHOUSE KICK — HEEL KICK: OPEN STANCE

(1—3) Slide rear foot to front foot. (4) Simultaneously lift rear foot from the ground, roll hips to twist leg to a 45-degree angle and fold. (5) Snap a roundhouse kick to the opponent's groin with the ball of the foot. (6) Retract kick to the 45-degree angle fold. (7) Snap kicking foot behind opponent's back. (8) Reverse direction of the kicking leg by rolling the kicking hip over in the direction of your opponent. (9) Strike the opponent at the base of the skull with your heel. (10) Follow the direction and force of the kick by snapping the heel into your thigh.

1

4

7

8

DEFENSIVE ROUNDHOUSE KICK — SIDE KICK: OPEN STANCE

This position is for defense against an aggressive fighter or a counterattacker. (1) Align your centerline with your opponent's centerline. (2) Lift front foot to a high horizontal fold position, simultaneously twisting the hip and turning the supporting heel to your opponent. (3) Snap the ball of your foot to your opponent's head. The opponent evades by blocking or dodging. (4&5) Immediately withdraw the kicking foot to the supporting ankle, twisting your hips toward him as he attacks. (6—8) Drive a side kick into your opponent's groin or solar plexus. Keep the kneecap facing the ground for maximum hip commitment. (9&10) Snap kick back to knee in the event of a second or continued attack. (11) Return to fighting position.

2

3

6

7

10

11

FAKE
ROUNDHOUSE KICK —
HEEL KICK:
CLOSED STANCE

(1—3) Move rear foot to front position. (4) Simultaneously lift rear foot, roll hip and fold kicking leg to a 45-degree angle. (5&6) Snap roundhouse kick into the back of your opponent's knee with your instep. (7) Withdraw kicking foot to the 45-degree angle fold. (8) Snap kicking foot in front of your opponent in a "second roundhouse kick motion" at thigh level. (9) Snap the kick back toward your opponent, arcing your heel toward his throat, and roll the hip. Twist the heel of the supporting foot to point past your opponent's back to insure maximum contact. (10&11) Complete the kicking motion by snapping your heel into your thigh. (12) Re-establish fighting position.

ROUNDHOUSE KICK —
SIDE KICK:
OPEN STANCE

(1) Align your centerline of balance with your opponent's centerline of balance. (2&3) Employ the extended fold position. (4) Attempt a roundhouse kick to the back of your opponent's head. The kick scores, misses or is blocked. (5) Return kicking leg to the fold. (6) Assume beginning stance. (7) Recreate the exact, extended fold position, drawing your opponent's attention to the same fold which just produced a roundhouse kick. As your kicking calf begins movement, your opponent throws up his front arm in anticipation of a high roundhouse. (8) Drive a side kick into your opponent's ribs. (9) Return kick to fold. (10) Assume beginning stance.

SIDE KICK —
ROUNDHOUSE KICK:
OPEN STANCE

(1) Align your centerline of balance with your opponent's centerline of balance. (2) Employ the extended fold position. (3) Execute a side kick into your opponent's rib cage. The kick will score, miss or be blocked. (4) Return the kicking leg to the fold. (5) Assume beginning stance. (6&7) Recreate the exact, extended fold position, drawing your opponent's attention to the same fold which just produced a side kick. (8) As your kicking leg begins movement, your opponent drops his front arm, anticipating the low side kick. (9) Snap a roundhouse kick to the opponent's unguarded head. (10) Snap kick back to fold. (11) Re-establish beginning balance.

1

4

5

8

9

2

3

6

7

10

11

KICKING for SELF-DEFENSE

In the introduction, I stated that all of the combinations in this text are functional for tournament competition and self-defense. Many of the techniques demonstrated are designed to be used against trained and sophisticated fighters. Frankly, they would be wasted on the majority of street fighters.

The easiest method of bringing an attacker under control during the self-defense situation is to kick to the knees, thighs, groin, shins and to stomp the feet. On the street it is important to hit first, fast and very hard. A kick executed to the lower body area is

easy to initiate and produces immediate results. A kick delivered
to the throat or head is always a surprise to an attacker untrained
in the martial arts. For that reason, do not rule out the possibility
of high kicks for self-defense.

Punching techniques are included with kicking moves to make
the self-defense techniques realistic. Remember that punches set
up an opponent for a kicking attack, and kicks set up an opponent
for a punching attack. A few common self-defense situations have
been presented with specific defensive counters.

DEFENSE AGAINST
TWO-HANDED GRAB

(1&2) Pin your opponent's hand to yourself to prevent his retreat or control of your balance. (3) Simultaneously drop your kicking foot to the rear in a strong stance. (4&5) Snap the shin or instep of the foot into your attacker's groin. (6) Snap the kicking foot back to the supporting knee. (7) Return the kicking foot to the deep stance and prepare to follow up if necessary.

2

4

5

7

SECOND DEFENSE
AGAINST A CLOSE
TWO-HANDED GRAB

(1&2) Clap both of your hands on your opponent's ears, breaking the ear drums. (3&4) Grab the ears or hair on the back of the attacker's head and drive your forehead into the bridge of your opponent's nose. (5&6) Snap your knee into your opponent's groin.

DEFENSE
AGAINST A FULL NELSON

(1—3) Drive a back kick into your opponent's knee. (4&5) Scrape the shin with the side of the foot, stomping the instep. (6) Move your hips to the side. (7) Drive a chop into the attacker's groin.

2

4

5

7

DEFENSE AGAINST AN ARM BAR

(1) Attacker holds your right arm behind your back, forcing your hand up against the elbow and shoulder joints. (2—5) Drive your elbow into your opponent's ribs several times. (6) Bend forward quickly. (7) Twist a full 180-degrees to the corresponding direction of the arm which is trapped. (If the right arm is pinned, twist to the right.) (8) Gain control of your opponent's position by bending the palm of his controlling hand toward his elbow, and simultaneously twist the hand away from you. (9—11) Drive a front snap kick into the attacker's groin.

1

4

5

8

9

DEFENSE AGAINST
A STRAIGHT PUNCH

(1—4) As your opponent punches, side step with your front foot and parry the punch with the front hand. (5&6) Quickly grab the punching arm with the rear hand while folding the rear leg for a kick. (7) Drive a roundhouse kick into the attacker's groin, using the instep as the weapon.

DEFENSE
AGAINST A STRAIGHT, LUNGING PUNCH

(1—4) As your opponent punches, side step with the front foot and parry the punch with the front hand. (5&6) Quickly grab the punching arm with the rear hand while folding the rear leg for a kick. (7) Drive a roundhouse kick into your opponent's groin, using the instep as a weapon. (8) Snap the foot back to your knee. (9—11) Thrust side kick to the back of your opponent's knee, driving him to the ground. (12&13) Grab the back of your opponent's head by the hair and violently jerk his head back. (14&15) Deliver a downward elbow smash to the bridge of the attacker's nose.

DEFENSE AGAINST A WILD ROUNDHOUSE PUNCH

(1—3) Stop the attacker's punch with an inside-to-outside block. (4&5) Snap a hard punch with the rear hand directly between the attacker's eyes. (6&7) Fold for a front snap kick from the rear leg. (8) Drive the instep or shin of your foot into your opponent's groin. (9) Snap the kick back to fold and return to initial position. (10) As your opponent doubles over, grab the back of his head. (11) Drive a knee into the attacker's face.